GREAT PRO SPORTS CHAMPIONSHIPS

GREAT FIFA WORLD CUP MATCHES

by Ethan Olson

BrightPoint Press

San Diego, CA

© 2024 BrightPoint Press
an imprint of ReferencePoint Press, Inc.
Printed in the United States

For more information, contact:
BrightPoint Press
PO Box 27779
San Diego, CA 92198
www.BrightPointPress.com

ALL RIGHTS RESERVED.

No part of this work covered by the copyright hereon may be reproduced or used in any form or by any means—graphic, electronic, or mechanical, including photocopying, recording, taping, web distribution, or information storage retrieval systems—without the written permission of the publisher.

LIBRARY OF CONGRESS CATALOGING-IN-PUBLICATION DATA

Names: Olson, Ethan, author.
Title: Great FIFA World Cup matches / by Ethan Olson.
Description: San Diego, CA: BrightPoint, [2024] | Series: Great pro sports championships | Includes bibliographical references and index. | Audience: Ages 13 | Audience: Grades 7–9
Identifiers: LCCN 2023015134 (print) | LCCN 2023015135 (eBook) | ISBN 9781678206529 (hardcover) | ISBN 9781678206536 (eBook)
Subjects: LCSH: World Cup (Soccer)--Juvenile literature. | Soccer matches--Juvenile literature. | Soccer--History--Juvenile literature. | Maradona, Diego, 1960-2020--Juvenile literature. | Messi, Lionel, 1987---Juvenile literature.
Classification: LCC GV943.49 .O45 2024 (print) | LCC GV943.49 (eBook) | DDC 796.334/668--dc23/eng/20230403
LC record available at https://lccn.loc.gov/2023015134
LC eBook record available at https://lccn.loc.gov/2023015135

CONTENTS

AT A GLANCE	4
INTRODUCTION THE WORLD'S GAME	6
CHAPTER ONE THE WORLD CUP COMES HOME	10
CHAPTER TWO THE MAGIC OF MARADONA	22
CHAPTER THREE INSPIRING A NATION	34
CHAPTER FOUR MESSI'S MOMENT	46
Glossary	58
Source Notes	59
For Further Research	60
Index	62
Image Credits	63
About the Author	64

AT A GLANCE

- The Fédération Internationale de Football Association (FIFA) first organized a men's World Cup in 1930. It has been played every four years since with two exceptions. The 1942 and 1946 tournaments were canceled because of World War II (1939–1945).

- The first Women's World Cup was played in 1991. It has continued every four years since.

- The men's World Cup is widely considered the most-watched sporting event on Earth. Roughly 1.5 billion people watched the final in 2022.

- The 1966 World Cup featured the hosts, England, against a talented West Germany team. England, the country where soccer was created, won the trophy for the first time in the nation's history.

- In 1986, Argentina was led by superstar forward Diego Maradona. He made himself a legend on the way to beating West Germany in the final.

- The 2011 Women's World Cup final saw the United States upset by a Japan team trying to lift its nation's spirits after a massive earthquake.

- France was defending its 2018 title at the 2022 men's final. It came up short against Argentina. The Argentines were led by the legendary Lionel Messi.

INTRODUCTION

THE WORLD'S GAME

On December 18, 2022, Argentina was pulling away from France in the men's World Cup final. The Argentines were already up 1–0. Legendary forward Lionel Messi had scored on a 23rd-minute **penalty kick**. They made it 2–0 a few minutes before halftime. A quick

counterattack put Argentina midfielder Alexis Mac Allister clear through on goal. Mac Allister spotted winger Ángel Di Maria sprinting down the other wing. After a quick pass from Mac Allister, Di Maria tapped the ball into the net.

Kylian Mbappé scored eight goals during the 2022 men's World Cup.

French star Kylian Mbappé still believed France could win going into halftime. He dug into his teammates in the locker room. "Get into the one-on-ones and change things, guys. It's a World Cup final. We are two goals down. We can come back!" he said.[1] It was exactly what the French team needed to hear.

THE WORLD'S BIGGEST STAGE

Matchups between soccer's best teams, including Argentina and France, have made the men's World Cup the world's most viewed sporting event. An estimated

Mbappé competes with Argentina's Lionel Messi for the ball during the 2022 men's World Cup final.

5.4 billion people tuned in at some point during the 2022 men's tournament. Fans watch to see the greatest stars in the sport perform on the biggest stage in the world.

1
THE WORLD CUP COMES HOME

People have been playing soccer-like games for thousands of years. But it was in the 1800s in England that the modern rules were first created. The country liked to say it invented the sport. From there, soccer spread quickly around the globe.

By 1966, England still called itself the home of soccer. But it had never won the World Cup. Now hosting the tournament, the national team players felt huge pressure to get the victory.

England had a great team. Captain Bobby Moore was a star defender.

England (in red) and West Germany line up before the start of the 1966 World Cup final.

Bobby Charlton was the team's creative midfielder. Forward Jimmy Greaves was one of the world's best scorers. England won its group, then won two knockout games to reach the final. But along the way Greaves was hurt. His place was taken in the lineup by Geoff Hurst.

THE HEIST

Four months before the 1966 tournament, the World Cup trophy was stolen from its display case in London. It was found a week later in a hedge by a man named David Corbett. His dog, Pickles, smelled the trophy, which was wrapped in newspaper. Corbett and Pickles were treated as national heroes. Both were invited to the team's banquet after the tournament.

West Germany had won the World Cup in 1954. In 1966, it rolled into the final behind strikers Uwe Seeler and Helmut Haller. Young midfielder Franz Beckenbauer was also becoming one of the best players in the world.

A FAST START

The crowd of over 90,000 fans at London's famous Wembley Stadium included Queen Elizabeth II. The noisy arena went quiet just twelve minutes into the game when Haller scored for West Germany. Hurst then tied the game six minutes later.

England goalkeeper Gordon Banks (left) fails to stop a shot from West Germany's Helmut Haller (far right) in the first half.

The rest of the first half produced chances on both sides. But both goalkeepers played well. England's Gordon Banks and West Germany's Hans Tilkowski both came up with big saves. The score was still 1–1 at halftime.

THE DUEL

An interesting battle grew as the game went along. Beckenbauer was a great attacking player. He had scored West Germany's winner in the semifinals. On the other side, Charlton had scored both of England's semifinal goals in a 2–1 win.

Before the match, England manager Alf Ramsay asked Charlton to focus less on offense. Ramsay wanted Charlton to cover Beckenbauer wherever the West German star went. Oddly, West German manager Helmut Schön had given Beckenbauer similar instructions. Schön wanted

England's Bobby Charlton (left) and West Germany's Franz Beckenbauer (right) were two of soccer's best players in the 1960s.

Beckenbauer to cover Charlton. The two superstars followed each other all game. Neither one was very useful on offense.

The goals had to come from other places. In the 78th minute, England midfielder Martin Peters picked up a deflection. He beat Tilkowski with a low, hard shot to put England in front.

Time was running out. As the seconds ticked away, the crowd grew louder and louder. Then in the game's final minute, West Germany scored. The ball dropped to Wolfgang Weber off another deflection. He smashed it into the net from close range.

IN OR OUT?

That meant the game would go to extra time. The teams would play two full fifteen-minute halves, no matter who scored. Nearing the end of the first half,

Hurst collected a cross six yards from goal. His shot struck the crossbar and bounced straight down. It then spun back toward the field.

No one was sure if the ball had actually crossed the line. The referee, Gottfried Dienst, had to check with his assistant on the sideline. After a discussion, the two men said the ball had gone in. To this day, many of the West German players are sure it was not a goal.

Despite the protest, the game moved on with England leading 3–2. As the game approached the 120-minute mark, both

Geoff Hurst fires his hat trick goal in the final seconds of extra time to put England up 4–2.

teams were exhausted. But the fans were overjoyed. They knew that England was close to winning. Several fans started to drift onto the field.

Some of the players seemed to stop when they saw the fans. But the game was still going. In the confusion, Moore sent a long pass forward to Hurst. The forward gathered the ball at midfield and sprinted in on goal.

Calling the match for English TV was legendary broadcaster Kenneth Wolstenholme. "And here comes Hurst. He's got . . . some people are on the **pitch**. They think it's all over!" Wolstenholme exclaimed. At that moment, Hurst blasted a shot into the West German net to make it 4–2. "It is now!" Wolstenholme added.[2]

With that, Hurst became the first player to ever score a **hat trick** in the men's World Cup final. No one would match the feat for

England captain Bobby Moore holds up the Jules Rimet Trophy as his teammates carry him off the field.

another fifty-six years. More importantly, it sealed the win for England.

2
THE MAGIC OF MARADONA

By the start of the 1986 World Cup, everyone knew who the world's best player was. Diego Maradona of Argentina was short, with broad shoulders. He needed to be strong. On those shoulders he carried the weight of his soccer-crazed country.

Maradona could handle the pressure. His dribbling skills were the best most fans had ever seen. His play excited fans during Argentina's run to the World Cup final in Mexico City, Mexico.

Argentina's Diego Maradona (left) takes on an England defender during the teams' quarterfinal game.

Maradona makes a run up the field in the semifinals against Belgium.

Maradona was also a clever player. All of his skills were on display against England in the quarterfinal. He scored Argentina's first goal by beating England goalie Peter

Shilton to a ball in the air and heading it in. Replays showed that Maradona had actually punched the ball in with his hand. Maradona's hand was close to his face. The referees didn't spot the foul. When asked about the goal, Maradona gave a famous answer: "The goal was scored a little bit with the head of Diego and a little with the hand of God."[3] It became known as the "Hand of God" goal.

Later in the game, Maradona picked up the ball in his own half. He dribbled past six English defenders at full speed. He then shot the ball into the net for the game-winning goal. That amazing run was later named the "Goal of the Century."

The Argentines then beat Belgium in the semifinals. Maradona again scored both of his team's goals. More than 114,000 fans showed up for the final at the Azteca Stadium in Mexico City to see what he would do next.

BUILDING THE LEAD

West German coach Franz Beckenbauer had a plan for Maradona. Young midfielder Lothar Matthäus would follow Argentina's star all game. If Beckenbauer's plan

West German defenders Karlheinz Förster (4) and Lothar Matthäus tackle Maradona during the first half of the final.

worked, West Germany could win the World Cup for the third time.

Early on, Matthäus frustrated Maradona. The Argentine even picked up a yellow card in the 17th minute. But in the 23rd minute,

German goalkeeper Harald Schumacher came out to play a free kick cross and missed the ball. Argentina's José Luis Brown headed it into the open net for a 1–0 lead.

The game stayed that way until Argentina broke forward quickly in the 56th minute.

FRANZ BECKENBAUER

The 1986 loss made West Germany manager Franz Beckenbauer the first man to ever lose a World Cup final as both a manager and a player. But he had also won the tournament as a player in 1974. In 1990, he led West Germany to a 1–0 victory over Argentina in the final. That made Beckenbauer just the second man to ever win the tournament both ways.

Midfielder Héctor Enrique slipped a pass to Jorge Valdano. The forward was suddenly one-on-one with Schumacher. He hit a low shot that beat the goalkeeper, and it was 2–0.

CORNERED

West Germany needed a break. It took until the 74th minute to find one. A corner kick was deflected off the head of forward Rudi Völler at the near post. It fell to captain Karl-Heinz Rummenigge a few yards from goal. Rummenigge beat two defenders to the ball. He scored to make it 2–1.

Jorge Burruchaga (7) scores the winning goal for Argentina.

Just seven minutes later, West Germany had another corner. This one was kicked long, toward the far post. West German defender Thomas Berthold headed it back to the micdle. Völler smacked it in.

Argentina had been trying to slow the game down when it was ahead. Now it had to turn the tempo back up. Luckily, Argentina had just the man to do it. Maradona finally found some room in the 85th minute. He picked the ball up near the midfield line, with space. It was about the same spot from which he had started his famous run against England. Knowing that, a handful of West German defenders closed in.

Maradona gathered the ball with one touch, then popped it ahead to midfielder Jorge Burruchaga. Everyone had been focused on Maradona. No one was back to defend for West Germany. Burruchaga raced in on goal. West German defender Hans-Peter Briegel tried to chase him down. Just before the defender got there, Burruchaga tapped the ball past Schumacher and into the net.

The late goal ended up making the difference. The victory secured Argentina's second World Cup title. It was the only one Maradona would ever win. But his performances in the 1986 tournament are still remembered as some of the best ever.

Maradona holds up the World Cup trophy during Argentina's victory celebration on the field.

3
INSPIRING A NATION

On March 11, 2011, a powerful earthquake rumbled under the ocean 80 miles (128 km) off the coast of Sendai, Japan. It caused a huge **tsunami** to crash over the shores of the island nation. The flooding killed more than 18,000 people and injured nearly 9,000 others. It also caused a meltdown at the Fukushima nuclear power plant. The tragedy cost an estimated $235 billion for recovery. It was the most expensive disaster in world history.

While the country rebuilt, the Japanese soccer team traveled to Germany in June.

Rachel Buehler (left) of the United States battles for the ball with Japan's Aya Miyama in the 2011 Women's World Cup final.

They were there for the 2011 Women's World Cup. At the time, Japan did not even have a fully professional league for women. Japan had skilled players. But few experts expected the nation to win.

Germany came into the tournament as a favorite. It was the two-time defending champion. But Japan shocked

FINDING MOTIVATION

Japan manager Norio Sasaki motivated his team against Germany with a slideshow. It had images of the damage from the earthquake and tsunami. The team eventually won the match on a goal by forward Karina Muruyama in the 108th minute.

the Germans 1–0 in the quarterfinals. Japan then beat Sweden to set up a matchup with the United States in the final. Along the way, the Japanese media latched on to the team as a beacon of hope.

AN EVEN BATTLE

Like Germany, the United States was one of the sport's top teams. The Americans had won the 1991 and 1999 World Cups. The team featured superstars such as forward Abby Wambach and goalie Hope Solo. And after a dramatic quarterfinal win over Brazil, they came into the final with momentum.

Hope Solo stops a penalty kick during the United States' quarterfinal win over Brazil.

The United States had usually dominated Japan. That looked like it would continue early in the match. American midfielder Lauren Cheney came within inches of a goal off winger Megan Rapinoe's cross. In the 28th minute, a shot from Wambach hit the crossbar. But it was still 0–0 at halftime.

US coach Pia Sundhage brought on young forward Alex Morgan at the break. Within three minutes, Morgan had also hit the post. In the 68th minute, Morgan took a long pass from Rapinoe. Morgan outraced a defender and buried a hard shot into the bottom corner.

The Japanese team was known for playing a smart, organized style. That defensive focus had paid off early. But after Morgan's goal, they had to push forward. In the 80th minute, the United States failed to clear a low cross. Japan forward Aya Miyama jumped on a loose ball. She tied

Abby Wambach (20) heads in a goal to put the United States up 2–1.

the match with a point-blank shot. The teams went to a thirty-minute extra time. The first half was nearly over when Morgan outdueled two Japanese defenders in the corner. She drilled a cross to Wambach, who scored from close range. It was Wambach's record-breaking thirteenth goal all-time in World Cup play.

All tournament long, Japan had been led by midfielder Homare Sawa. The team captain was one of the world's best players. She had four goals entering the final. That total was the most of any player in the tournament. In the 116th minute, Sawa raced out to meet a corner kick by the near post. With her back to goal, she kicked the ball with her heel. The shot beat Solo and went into the net. The goal sent the stadium into a wild celebration.

ON THE LINE

It was the second Women's World Cup final to reach a penalty shootout. The United States had beaten China that way in 1999. But that game had been scoreless when the shootout started. The 2011 final had four goals already. Fans at the Waldstadion in Frankfurt, Germany, knew they were witnessing the most exciting women's final ever.

Japan goalkeeper Ayumi Kaihori had already come up with many big saves. She started the shootout with another stop. Kaihori actually dived past Shannon

Japan goalkeeper Ayumi Kaihori reaches back with her foot to stop a penalty shootout attempt from the United States' Shannon Boxx.

Boxx's shot. She reached back and saved it with her foot.

Miyama scored, putting Japan ahead. That brought up US forward Carli Lloyd. Normally a clutch scorer, she sailed her shot over the crossbar.

The teams then traded stops and goals, and Japan led 2–1. But the Japanese had two shots left. The United States had only one. If Saki Kumagai could score, the match would be over.

Solo wasn't going to make it easy. The American stood a few yards in front of the goal, swinging her arms. She was trying to throw off Kumagai's rhythm. It didn't work. When the whistle blew, Kumagai hammered an unstoppable shot high into the corner. Solo dived the right way. But she couldn't reach it. Japanese players flooded onto the field to celebrate.

Japan in 2011 became the first Asian country to ever win a World Cup.

No Asian team, men's or women's, had ever lifted the World Cup trophy. And before the tournament, few experts had given Japan a chance. But even the Americans knew Japan's run was special. "We lost to a great team, we really did," Solo said after the game. "I truly believe that something bigger was pulling for this team."[4]

4
MESSI'S MOMENT

Through six games at the 2022 men's World Cup, Lionel Messi had scored five goals for Argentina. With each performance, his play seemed to be willing his team to victory. Messi had a reason to be inspired. He had won many trophies. But he had never won the World Cup.

At thirty-five years old, this was likely Messi's last chance. To many fans, that was the one thing holding Messi back. With a

Lionel Messi appeared in his fifth World Cup in 2022.

win, he could join Brazil's Pelé and fellow Argentinian Diego Maradona as one of the best players of all time. Each had led their country to the sport's biggest prize.

Standing in Argentina's way was the brightest star of the next generation. Four years earlier, Kylian Mbappé had led France to the 2018 World Cup title as a teenager. Now the speedy winger had

LEAVING A MARK

Lionel Messi scored a goal in each of the 2010, 2014, 2018, and 2022 tournaments. That made him only the fourth man to score in four World Cups.

Ángel Di Maria celebrates after putting Argentina ahead 2–0 in the first half.

the talented French team ready to win back-to-back titles.

The crowd inside Lusail Stadium in Lusail, Qatar, was mostly Argentina fans. Even worse for France, several members of the team had been sick during the week.

The French players looked tired at the beginning of the match. Argentina looked fresh. After Argentine winger Ángel Di Maria drew a foul in the box, Messi scored on a 23rd-minute penalty kick. Argentina went up 2–0 in the 36th minute. This time Di Maria finished off a quick counterattack.

TURNING THE TIDE

French manager Didier Deschamps was desperate. In an uncommon move, he even substituted two players before halftime. Nothing seemed to work. It was still 2–0 at halftime. The French looked finished. At the

MOST GOALS IN MEN'S WORLD CUP HISTORY*

⚽	Miroslav Klose, Germany	16
⚽	Ronaldo, Brazil	15
⚽	Gerd Müller, West Germany	14
⚽	Just Fontaine, France	13
⚽	Lionel Messi, Argentina	13
⚽	Kylian Mbappé, France	12
⚽	Pelé, Brazil	12

*Through 2022

Source: "All-Time Top Goalscorers World Cup," Transfermarkt, n.d. www.transfermarkt.us.

Both Lionel Messi and Kylian Mbappé are among the all-time leading World Cup scorers.

break, Deschamps told French TV, "[The players] have to fight."[5]

It was still 2–0 with ten minutes left. Suddenly, the French sprang to life.

Randal Kolo Muani, one of the early substitutes, was fouled in the box. Mbappé scored the penalty kick past Argentine goalkeeper Emiliano Martinez.

The goal inspired France. Less than a minute later, Mbappé got under a cross-field pass. He then traded passes with teammate Marcus Thuram on the edge of the **penalty area**. Mbappé finished the move by hammering a **volley** past Martinez.

A few minutes earlier, the game seemed over. Now it was tied. Messi had one more chance before the second half ended. Dribbling just outside the area, he suddenly

Mbappé fires a shot to tie the game 2–2 late in the second half.

let go a high, hard shot. Only the stretched arm of French goalie Hugo Lloris kept it out.

EXTRA MAGIC

The first half of extra time passed without a goal. In the 108th minute, Argentina burst forward. Striker Lautaro Martinez blasted a shot off Lloris's palms. The rebound bounced straight to Messi, just a few yards from goal. French defender Joules Koundé was standing near the goal line. He appeared to block Messi's shot. But the ball had crossed the line by the time it hit Koundé.

Argentina led 3–2. But with four minutes left, defender Gonzalo Montiel hit the ball with his hand inside the Argentina penalty area. Mbappé stepped up to take the penalty kick. He once again beat Martinez. The young forward had scored just the second men's World Cup final hat trick ever.

Argentina goalkeeper Emiliano Martinez (right) leaps in celebration after stopping a shot from France's Kingsley Coman (left) in the penalty shootout.

The game went to a penalty shootout. Mbappé and Messi took the first kicks for each country. They both scored.

Despite not saving any of Mbappé's three attempts, Martinez was considered a great penalty stopper. He liked to play mind games with shooters. As France's Kingsley Coman approached the penalty spot, Martinez taunted the winger. He then stuffed Coman's shot.

After Paulo Dybala put Argentina ahead, Martinez tried another trick. He picked the ball up and threw it away from the penalty spot. The referee gave Martinez a yellow card for his behavior. But after Aurélien Tchouaméni missed wide, Martinez danced in celebration.

The next two penalty takers scored. Argentina could win it with a successful kick. Montiel stepped up for a chance to

Messi (with trophy) led Argentina to its third men's World Cup title in 2022.

make up for his handball. He hit the corner with his shot. The Argentine fans went wild.

It was Argentina's first win since 1986. Messi had scored seven goals in the tournament and finally won it. It cemented his place as one of the sport's true legends.

GLOSSARY

counterattack

when a team regains possession and immediately attacks the opponent with speed

hat trick

when a player scores three goals in a game

penalty area

a large rectangular area extended around the goal at each end of the field

penalty kick

a free kick from the penalty spot awarded to the attacking team after a foul within the penalty area

pitch

another name for a soccer field

tsunami

a large wave caused by a volcanic eruption or an earthquake

volley

a kick that is taken when the ball is falling out of the air

SOURCE NOTES

INTRODUCTION: THE WORLD'S GAME

1. Quoted in Jacob Whitehead and Dominic Fifield, "Mbappe's France Half-time Speech: 'Either We Let Them Play Us Like Idiots or We Change Things!,'" *The Athletic*, December 21, 2022. www.theathletic.com.

CHAPTER ONE: THE WORLD CUP COMES HOME

2. Quoted in "Original Broadcast, 1966 World Cup Final," *YouTube*, uploaded by ClassicEngland, April 27, 2012. www.youtube.com.

CHAPTER TWO: THE MAGIC OF MARADONA

3. Quoted in "Factbox: Maradona's Most Famous Quotes," *Reuters*, November 25, 2020. www.reuters.com.

CHAPTER THREE: INSPIRING A NATION

4. Quoted in Reuters, "Japan Had Something Bigger on Its Side: Solo," *Reuters*, July 17, 2011. www.reuters.com.

CHAPTER FOUR: MESSI'S MOMENT

5. Quoted in Sam Rooke, "Didier Deschamps in TV Rant on France's First-Half Display in World Cup Final–'We Utterly Failed to Show Up,'" *Eurosport*, December 18, 2022. www.eurosport.com.

FOR FURTHER RESEARCH

BOOKS

Thomas Carothers, *Women's World Cup Heroes*. Minneapolis, MN: Abdo Publishing, 2019.

Lesa Cline-Ransome, *Not Playing by the Rules: 21 Female Athletes Who Changed Sports*. New York: Alfred A. Knopf, 2020.

David Stabler, *Meet Lionel Messi*. Minneapolis, MN: Lerner Publications, 2022.

INTERNET SOURCES

Paul Brown, "World Cup 1966: They Think It's All Over: How the 1966 World Cup Helped Save English Soccer," *Medium*, May 23, 2018. www.medium.com.

Chris Hunt, "Olé! The Chaotic Story Behind a 1986 World Cup Which Had Everything," *FourFourTwo*, June 3, 2014. www.fourfourtwo.com.

"Japan's Emotional 2011 World Cup Success Remembered," *FIFA*, July 17, 2021. www.fifa.com.

WEBSITES

FBRef
https://fbref.com

FBRef is a research website that offers statistical data for national and club teams as well as current and former players.

FIFA
www.fifa.com

The website for FIFA contains information on world soccer's governing body as well as details about all men's and women's World Cup tournaments, past and future.

US Soccer
www.ussoccer.com

The website for the US Soccer Federation contains detailed information on the country's men's and women's national teams.

INDEX

Banks, Gordon, 14
Beckenbauer, Franz, 13, 15–16, 26, 28
Berthold, Thomas, 30
Boxx, Shannon, 42–43
Briegel, Hans-Peter, 32
Brown, José Luis, 28
Burruchaga, Jorge, 31–32

Charlton, Bobby, 12, 15–16
Cheney, Lauren, 38
Coman, Kingsley, 56

Di Maria, Ángel, 7, 50
Dybala, Paulo, 56

Enrique, Héctor, 29

Greaves, Jimmy, 12

Haller, Helmut, 13
Hurst, Geoff, 12–13, 17, 20

Kaihori, Ayumi, 42
Kolo Muani, Randal, 52
Koundé, Joules, 54
Kumagai, Saki, 44

Lloris, Hugo, 53–54
Lloyd, Carli, 43

Mac Allister, Alexis, 7
Maradona, Diego, 22–27, 31–32, 48

Martinez, Emiliano, 52, 54–56
Martinez, Lautaro, 53
Matthäus, Lothar, 26–27
Mbappé, Kylian, 8, 48, 51, 52, 54–55
Messi, Lionel, 6, 46–47, 48, 50, 52, 54–55, 57
Miyama, Aya, 39, 43
Montiel, Gonzalo, 54, 56
Moore, Bobby, 11, 19
Morgan, Alex, 39–40
Muruyama, Karina, 36

Pelé, 48
Peters, Martin, 16

Rapinoe, Megan, 38–39
Rummenigge, Karl-Heinz, 29

Sawa, Homare, 41
Schumacher, Harald, 28–29, 32
Seeler, Uwe, 13
Shilton, Peter, 24–25
Solo, Hope, 37, 41, 44–45

Tchouaméni, Aurélien, 56,
Thuram, Marcus, 52
Tilkowski, Hans, 14, 17

Valdano, Jorge, 29
Völler, Rudi, 29–30

Wambach, Abby, 37, 38, 40–41
Weber, Wolfgang, 17

IMAGE CREDITS

Cover: © Petr David Josek/AP Images
5 (left): © Asatur Yesayants/Shutterstock Images
5 (right): © Romain Biard/Shutterstock Images
7: © Richard Callis/Fotoarena/Sipa USA/AP Images
9: © Laurent Zabulon/Abaca/Sipa USA/AP Images
11: © EMPPL PA Wire/AP Images
14: © EMPPL PA Wire/AP Images
16: © Sven Simon/picture-alliance/dpa/AP Images
19: © EMPPL PA Wire/AP Images
21: © EMPPL PA Wire/AP Images
23: © AP Images
24: © picture-alliance/dpa/AP Images
27: © picture-alliance/dpa/AP Images
30: © picture-alliance/dpa/AP Images
33: © Carlo Fumagalli/AP Images
35: © Thorsten Wagner/Getty Images Sport/Getty Images
38: © Jens Meyer/AP Images
40: © Thorsten Wagner/Getty Images Sport/Getty Images
43: © Marcio Jose Sanchez/AP Images
45: © Joern Pollex/Getty Images Sport/Getty Images
47: © Richard Callis/Fotoarena/Sipa USA/AP Images
49: © Laurent Zabulon/Abaca/Sipa USA/AP Images
51: © Red Line Editorial
53: © Laurent Zabulon/Abaca/Sipa USA/AP Images
55: © Richard Callis/Fotoarena/Sipa USA/AP Images
57: © Richard Callis/Fotoarena/Sipa USA/AP Images

ABOUT THE AUTHOR

Ethan Olson is a sportswriter and editor based in Minneapolis, Minnesota.